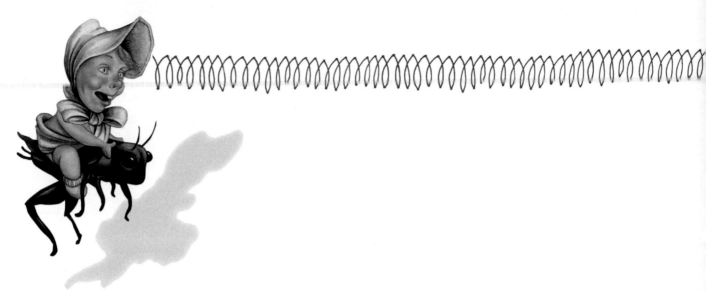

Rabbit Ears Books is an imprint of Rabbit Ears Entertainment, LLC.
29 North Main Street
South Norwalk, CT 06854

eBook edition 2011
ISBN 0-615-54771-8

paperback edition 2012
ISBN 978-1-939228-06-2

TOM THUMB

Written by Brad Kessler

Illustrated by Tim Gabor

Rabbit Ears Books

Most of you have heard full well of King Arthur and the Knights of the Round Table, how a long time ago in England King Arthur gathered at his court in Camelot the most courageous men of his day. Some of you might even know some of their names: there was Sir Lancelot, and Sir Galahad, and Sir Gawain.

But the bravest and noblest of them all was a little-known knight who all the histories through the ages overlooked. Yet without this very knight, King Arthur himself would surely have lost his crown.

OUR STORY STARTS IN THE STONE COTTAGE
of a poor farmer in the south of England. One day, the farmer's wife gave
birth to a son, quite hale and healthy, but alas, no larger than a human thumb.
And so his parents named him Tom Thumb.

Now the farmer and his wife loved the child more than
anything in the world. For what Tom Thumb lacked in size,
he tripled in spirit.

When he was but a fortnight old,
 Tom learned to saddle unsuspecting crickets
and ride them roughshod 'round the cottage.

Later, he taught himself to fly on the backs of butterflies and to wrestle honey bees — all of which made his parents exceedingly nervous, as they feared greatly for his safety.

So much did his parents wish to shelter Tom from harm, that they kept him in the cottage, away from the dangers of the much larger world. Whenever Tom asked if he could help in the fields, his father would say, "not today Tom, 'tis safer for ye at home."

  And whenever he asked to help at the market, his mother would say, "Not today Tom, 'tis best for ye at home."

  So day after day, Tom stayed behind at the house and watched as his parents made off to their chores.

One day, after his parents had left, Tom saw an
unforgettable sight.

Running through a meadow in front of the cottage, was a
young damsel fleeing a hideous dragon. Just as the dragon
was about to snatch the damsel, a knight in gleaming
armor burst from the wood, moving swiftly on his
steed with his lance lowered and steadied.

"I am a knight of the Round Table come
from Camelot, " the knight said
to the dragon.

"Give up yon damsel, and pledge
thyself to the Queen, otherwise
I shall run ye through
horn to hoof."

It didn't take long for the dragon to think well upon it. He let go of the
maiden, slumped to the ground with his tail between his legs, and
pledged himself to Queen Guinevere, weeping quite embarassingly
all the while.

Now little Tom had been watching this with eyes agape and mouth
awide, for the dragon was considerably larger than the knight,
yet the knight had countenanced no fear. So taken was Tom with
the knight's courage, that he resolved that he too would become
a knight of the Round Table.

The very next day, Tom sewed himself a suit of armor from the shells of beetles. He carved a helmet from an acorn crown and plumed it with the tail feather of a titmouse. He took one of his mother's sewing pins for a sword and sheathed it in a case stitched from pure spider web. And for several weeks, he practiced jousting and sword fighting, first, with an army of boisterous ants, and finally, with the family hamster.

At last, early one morning, he wrote his parents a note, saying, "I've gone off to King Arthur's court and promise I'll return," as soon as he became a knight but not before.

Then he slipped from the cottage and headed off to Camelot.

Now it was, assuredly, a long journey to Camelot for such a tiny lad as Tom. He walked through a field of towering barley grass, which he climbed occasionally to get his bearings. For lunch, he ate a whole wild red currant and then quenched his thirst with a drop of dew.

After dining, he set forth again. But no sooner had he walked sixty steps, than a great black raven swept down from the skies and snatched Tom by the seat of the pants!

The bird flew up and up, high above the treetops.
From up there, Tom could see forests and fields and far in the distance, his parents' cottage disappearing over the horizon.

Ere long, Tom said to the raven,

"Good raven, what do you plan
to do with me?"

"Well, you're the last ingredient for
me shepherd's pie," the raven replied.

Tom turned this over a bit and said,

"Wit thee well good raven, there's not much meat
on me you know."

"Never you mind," said the raven.

"And I'd likely cause you indigestion," said Tom.

"Ah go'on," said the raven.

"Indeed," said Tom. "Many a time I've been eaten by ravens just like you, and every time they've become sicker than hounds. But suit thyself. Eat me if you like."

Tom folded his arms and feigned such disinterest that it rattled the raven's confidence and he thought, perhaps, Tom was telling the truth.

So without further ado, the raven dropped Tom from his talons, and he tumbled down through the sky, head over heel over head, heels over head, and so on. Down, down he went until he landed with a great splash in the center of a small brook.

Before he knew it, Tom was washed down the stream, desperately bobbing about like a cork on the swift current. He grabbed hold of a passing maple leaf and threw himself aboard.

Now he was certain
he'd never reach
Camelot and never
become a knight.
So he laid down
on the leaf, exhausted,
and fell fast asleep.

When Tom awoke, evening was drawing nigh and the
sun was setting over a grassy meadow. He turned
around, and there before him stood a magnificent
castle. Its high turrets and towers thrust towards
the heavens, banners flapping smartly in the
breeze. He heard the blare of trumpets and realized
he could only be in Camelot!

He left his leaf and swam with all his might toward shore. Yet
before he got there, a water bearer dipped his bucket in the pond
and scooped up Tom, carrying him to the castle unawares. Soon
the water was poured into a pitcher and the pitcher placed on a
table. And Tom, who had been treading water all along, climbed out
of the pitcher and found himself straight in the center of the
Round Table!

He stood for a moment dripping wet and speechless, staring all around him. Stretching as far as Tom could see were great mountains of mutton chops, whole hillsides of pickled cabbage, pyramids of steaming potatoes and vast, savory pastures of Yorkshire pudding. Looming above this forest of fragrant food were men eating and drinking, belching and bragging, with jesters and squires and lute players by their sides. There was Sir Lancelot, and there Sir Galahad, and Sir Gawain. There Sir Cumference and Sir Tax and Sir Charge, and there Sir Tificate of Deposit, who was eating his food with the greatest of interest.

And staring straight down at Tom was none other than King Arthur himself.

"What's this?" King Arthur said, pointing towards Tom. The table fell instantly silent. All faces turned in astonishment towards little Tom.

"Come here young man," King Arthur said.

"What is thy name, and what doth thou desire here?"

Tom removed the helmet from his head and made a long deep bow.

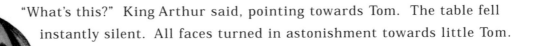

"I am, my lord, Tom Thumb, and I've come to thy court to become a knight."

With that, the table exploded into peals of uproarious laughter.

"Well bless my soul," said Sir Galahad, holding his gut with great mirth. "He wants to be a knight!"

"Look upon the fingerling," quoth Sir Gawain, "Why he couldn't even be an evening let alone a Knight!"

The men erupted once more into great cascades of laughter, and some began poking their fingers at Tom, while the table quaked and rocked with their merrymaking.

Just then, Queen Guinevere stepped toward the table and silenced the crowd with a nod of her head.

"Good sirs," said she. "Surely this is no manner for noble knights as ye to treat a guest of the Round Table. In truth, this Tom Thumb be small, but size is not the only measure of a man."

She cupped Tom in her hands and brought him close to her face and with a finger, fixed his helmet on his head. Tom blushed deeply, for Guinevere was a fine and passing beauty.

"Perhaps, he may prove himself worthy of knighthood one day," she said.

Then King Arthur raised his goblet and said, "Let us have a tournament for little Tom," to which a great cheer rose from the crowd.

So a crayfish was brought from the kitchen and the table cleared of its clutter. Guinevere gave Tom her colors to wear, as was the custom when Knights went into battle for their Ladies. And with a nod from Guinevere, the tournament began.

Now the crayfish was a nasty and terrible crustacean, at least twice the size of Tom. But Tom had practiced well in his parents' kitchen, and he parried and danced about, while the crayfish snapped its claws at the empty air.

But after a minute, the crayfish caught the heel
of Tom's boot and was dragging him about
the table.   Before it could squeeze him in
its claws, Tom unraveled the tiny thread of a nearby napkin and quickly tied
the crayfish's claws together in a tight knot.

"Very well Crayfish," Tom
said hopping on its back,
"Pledge thyself to the
Queen or I shall slay you."

Of course, the crayfish pledged itself to Guinevere and was promptly removed to the kitchen. And Tom was toasted all around as the tournament's hero.

And so Tom Thumb made a place for himself at the Round Table. Guinevere had the blacksmith make him a tiny suit of armor hammered from the finest silver, and she gave him a white mouse with a silk saddle. At the Round Table, he provided the knights with endless entertainment.

And though he was happy in Camelot, he hadn't, alas, been made a knight, and it greatly saddened him, for he could not go home and see his parents until he had fulfilled his promise to them.

One day after Arthur and the knights had gone to slay dragons in the north country, a messenger came to Guinevere and Tom with dire news.

The messenger related that King Arthur had been captured by the evil Black Knight and locked in his castle's dungeon. For several days, the Round Table knights had tried to set the king free, but had failed, and now hope was running out.

"We must make ready at once," Tom said to Guinevere. "Perhaps we can save him."

So Queen Guinevere put Tom in her pocket, and together they rode off on her palfrey for the north country.

In three days they arrived at the castle of the
Black Knight where Arthur was held captive. It
lay among leafless trees and craggy cliffs and a
low thick fog rolled unceasingly over the land.

The Black Knight was, in truth, a sorcerer who could make himself invisible
at will. He had an army of six thousand strong, with ninety-nine catapults
and countless cauldrons of bubbling oil to pour from the turret tops. He had
maces and burning arrows and balls of fire. The Round Table knights had
clearly met their match.

But Tom Thumb was not afraid. He unsheathed his
sewing pin and said,

"By my solemn oath, I shall save the King."

And before Guinevere could stop him, he charged
off, straight for the Black Knight's castle.

Now fortunately for Tom, he was too small for anyone to notice as he ran through the grass.   When he reached the castle's moat, he crossed quietly on a piece of twig. He climbed to the gate and slipped into the castle through a crack in the door.

Inside, scores of guards stood at the ready. Tom scurried around their feet as silently as a mouse and made his way down the dungeon steps. It was dark and the cold stone smelled of mildew and moss.

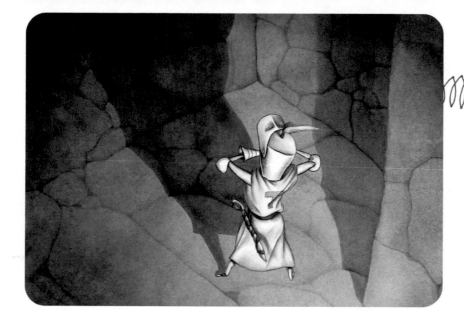

At the bottom, by the flicker of a single taper, he could see the dungeon door and two enormous guards with battle axes and broadswords at the ready.

Tom thought for a moment, then crept into a corner where his voice would echo the loudest. He took a deep breath and yelled as loud as he could.

"Guards come quick, upstairs. The Round Table knights have broken through!"

The guards heard the voice in the dimness and swung about, but couldn't see anyone standing there.

So Tom yelled again.

"Go on guards, don't stand there like blithering fools. Hie thee hence at once. Upstairs!"

The guards looked around again, this time stabbing blindly with their swords and swearing to themselves, until one of them finally said:

"Who's going there? Er... we can hear you, but can't see you."

And Tom replied,

"Who do you think goes here you thick-witted oafs. It is I, the
Black Knight, your Lord. I have made myself invisible for the
attack. Now get thee gone ninnies!"

With that, both guards begged pardon, slapped down their visors and lumbered upstairs.

When they were fully out of sight, Tom crept from his corner and scaled the dungeon door, using splinters and crags for footholds. He was just small enough to slip inside the keyhole, and once inside, he unsheathed his sewing

pin and placed it inside the lock. With a twist of his arm, the bolt unlatched, and the door swung open with a rusty creak.

"King Arthur," Tom whispered into the dark.

"Tom Thumb," the King said, emerging from the dark, "Is that you?"

"Yes, my lord. 'Tis I."

"Gramercy!" said Arthur, smiling broadly.

"'Tis a noble and courageous deed thee hath done."

And with that he placed Tom in his pocket, and the two stealthily escaped from the Black Knight's castle, under cover of fog.

When they returned to Arthur's castle, an enormous banquet was held in Tom's behalf, with all the Lords and Ladies of the kingdom in attendance. And a special escort was sent to Tom's parents' cottage to bring them to Camelot too.

When his parents entered the castle and saw Tom they rushed towards him in tears, happy to be reunited once again, their hearts swelled with pride.

And there, as his parents looked on, beaming from ear to ear, and as Guinevere lovingly clasped her hands, Tom knelt before the King. Slowly, the blade of Arthur's broadsword was brought down to touch Tom's tiny shoulders. The trumpets blared. The crowds gave shout, and Tom Thumb was officially declared the smallest and bravest knight ever to grace the kingdom of Camelot.

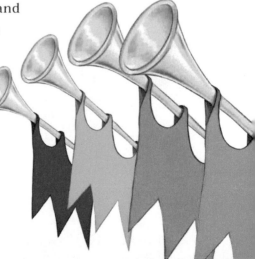